MEAT SONGS

AF071633

OTHER BOOKS FROM THE EMMA PRESS

POETRY ANTHOLOGIES

Slow Things: Poems about Slow Things
The Emma Press Anthology of Age
Mildly Erotic Verse
Urban Myths and Legends
The Emma Press Anthology of the Sea
This Is Not Your Final Form: Poems about Birmingham

POETRY COLLECTIONS FOR CHILDREN

Falling Out of the Sky: Poems about Myths and Monsters
Watcher of the Skies: Poems about Space and Aliens
Moon Juice, by Kate Wakeling
The Noisy Classroom, by Ieva Flamingo (July 2017)

THE EMMA PRESS PICKS

The Flower and the Plough, by Rachel Piercey
The Emmores, by Richard O'Brien
The Held and the Lost, by Kristen Roberts
Captain Love and the Five Joaquins, by John Clegg
Malkin, by Camille Ralphs
DISSOLVE to: L.A., by James Trevelyan
The Dragon and The Bomb, by Andrew Wynn Owen

POETRY PAMPHLETS

True Tales of the Countryside, by Deborah Alma
AWOL, by John Fuller and Andrew Wynn Owen
Goose Fair Night, by Kathy Pimlott
Mackerel Salad, by Ben Rogers
Trouble, by Alison Winch
Dragonish, by Emma Simon

Animal noises by Jack Nicholls
Illustrations by Mark Andrew Webber

THE EMMA PRESS

For Mum, Dad and Tom

ଔ

THE EMMA PRESS

First published in Great Britain in 2017
by the Emma Press Ltd

Text © Jack Nicholls 2017
Illustrations © Mark Andrew Webber 2017

All rights reserved.

The right of Jack Nicholls and Mark Andrew Webber to be identified as the author and illustrator respectively of this work has been asserted by them in accordance with the Copyright, Designs and Patents Act 1988.

ISBN 978-1-910139-62-2

A CIP catalogue record of this book
is available from the British Library.

Printed and bound in Great Britain
by Airdrie Print Services, Glasgow.

theemmapress.com
queries@theemmapress.com

CONTENTS

Headlouse 1
Grumpy Cat 2
Ground Mince Sonnet 5
Ants March on My Torso 6
Severed Pig's Head 8
Poem in Which I Sell You a Dog 9
In the Cat Café 11
Benson Laments the Loss of Hedges 12
Who's a Good Boy? 16
Caroline 17
White Tiger Farm 20
Hounds of Love 22
Our Cat, Cat, On Her Last Day 23
Baa 25

Acknowledgements 28
About the poet and illustrator 29
About the Emma Press 30

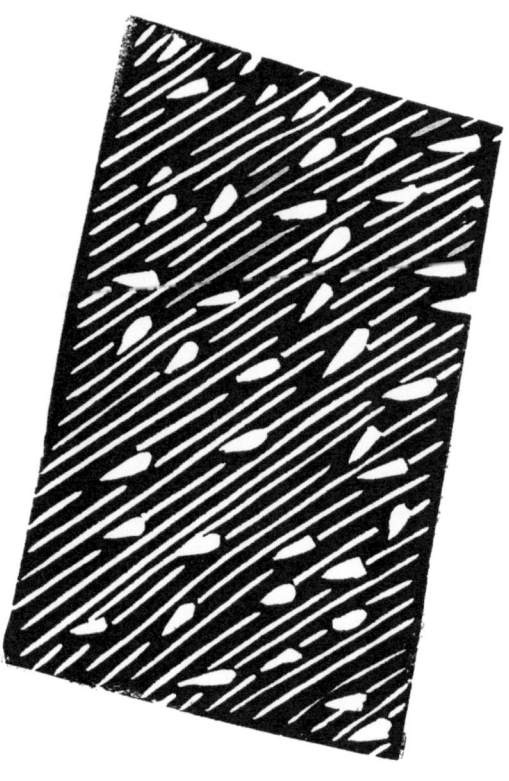

HEADLOUSE

I have only known the smell of you. Sometimes you poke a gaggy froth up here, the water beating, the air poison, but I hunker and I clasp I to a strand and still I smell it, the sweet and greasy smell of you.

I have eaten so much of you, I and all the other I, my teeming family. All your strands are heavy with us, the ground beneath us drained and divotted. Our frass, red and dirty, sticks to everything. My family scuttles under I and on I, pinching, all fingers and thumbs. It hurts when family enter I. I push out eggs and that hurts too. You send your hand to check on us. I do not know if you are enough.

Once when the froth came, sharp silver came too. Strands made murder. Harvested the eggs unthinking, dragged them to the shrieking cold, dragged family to the shrieking cold, split and stuck their bodies and everything was agony and you yourself was agony. I hunkered and I clasped. When it was over, not many of I were left and all family moved slowly from strand to strand and ate little mouthfuls, trembling. I felt peace in those few days before you filled again. It was you trying to care for I, or some of I.

You are family. I am as full of your blood as you are. I eat you hot and fresh, in kind thanks.

GRUMPY CAT

They line up one by one and hold their arms to me. I am the locus their fingers ache for. When I am alone I feel their ghosts and tingle to be held and brought to a room like this one. Finally – their fingers drag – yes – and then Oh, horrible, horrible.

Bring them to me. We are sick from not touching. I am all of their hearts, ready to curl up and yawn in their chests, and they are my bristling armour. Without them I am nude. They were born with me missing.

Bring them all. Let the days end with my muscles soggy and my skin an ill-fitting robe. Give us that second when we connect, electric, when we are phantom limbs locking into sockets, that sweet empty second before each of our itches returns.

Grant them these moments. Bring them forth. None shall go unhealed.

GROUND MINCE SONNET

Feels sweet to be a little worm, patted next to friends.
Every inch of us a blush to be as close as this.
They knitted us and now we puddle
a muddy us-mixture in our plastic carton.

In our blue days we never dreamed we'd be shucked
and garbled through machines, the parts of us
wrapped around the parts of us.
You might call this that we sing with pain,

but it's a raw and bloody thing, so why not love?
Did we ever press as close as now, did we know
one another with our skins on, do you know
what long bad night comes next? Why not love?

We sit on the shelf, pink mash of doomed souls.
Heart hugs gut hugs heart. Why not? Feels sweet.

ANTS MARCH ON MY TORSO

This piece will cost you eleven hundred dollars. I will go to any private place you choose and lie shirtless on the floor. Five hundred ants will walk in formation across my body. I will be the ground for them – me, my body, the flesh with my brain in it. You will be responsible for directing the ants towards me and I do not take responsibility for the ants if you find their movements unsatisfying. They are ants. The curve of my stomach will just be the way the land is for them, as will the depth of my navel and the sad dip in my chest that suggests the beginning of man breasts. The hair crawling from my genitalia to my navel will become an obstacle for five hundred ants to navigate. Please note that the setting of the piece must be private, as, shirtless, I will feel deeply ashamed. Regardless of audience I will

be alien, arbitrary, and in the way. I might move slightly and crush some of the ants, and the other ants will keep moving. This piece is not suitable for vegetarians. If, for example, my naked shoulder disintegrates an ant so totally that it is invisible to the human eye – save perhaps a faint stain on my skin – I will not notice. I will be the ground and the ground will not notice. I will not clean up crushed ants that need cleaning up. For an additional fee, I can make my bodily movements more erratic – I might have a coughing fit, or roll onto my front. It is not guaranteed that the ants will reroute or perish. You will be responsible for deciding whether the ants are suffering or triumphing ingeniously. The ants will walk and I will lie on the floor. This piece will not say anything new or make me feel better. You will provide the ants.

SEVERED PIG'S HEAD

After it all. Sucking and chewing up veggies and scum. Some of it the scum off us. And mum ripped away. All of her just a gone froth now in my mouth. A white taste just. And grey and gigantic in a hot shed. Pressing hard up to my family. Teeth knotted in our heads. Taking just the mud into myself sometimes on the black days. This need to swill something. The oil of body always touching another body. Pushing into others sometimes or getting pushed into. Saying here I am. Here you are. All grey tit all black slick unders. A gritting of your body mad but. After it all. Just a different closeness. Swilling a different mud. And never seeing another set of eyeballs. And asleepy then the machine and waking up with our heads off lop lop lop. My body off somewhere and this could have been any day. After my head in a jostling box cold and bloody with our other heads and then a tiny box for just mine and after being held by something warm and moist in a little shed noisy with not my family. Held tight by one while another took off his skins and all the others noised. And under his skins a flesh like ours but pinker. Coming near. His unders soft and raw. Him pushing in. For not much time but. And the noising. And finally I see eyeballs. So after it all is it surprising that they are blank and grey as the old shedwater? That I can't see a thing in them? They let me go and I hit the floor facing down and it could have been any day.

POEM IN WHICH I SELL YOU A DOG

Buy a dog body with a dogsoul in it.
You deserve to be licked and mauled
and you deserve a hungry muscular snaking
at your ankles, and you have money.

Oh, beautiful is the wallet bursting
to fill your stomach with a love
cold as milk, beautiful is the capital
sluiced into the animal that's yours!

I am gentle when I separate
the bodies from the dogs
you do not buy.

IN THE CAT CAFÉ

Hate you longhair whitehair
goldeyes you flatfaced you tongue
pink and ready you wrong smell
busy at the bowls you lapping
at the scratchers and singing
at the scratchers for scratches
you held thing you hugsoaked
you yawning with the others you
filling the little room with you
when the dark raps at the window
you ache in my stomach you plaything
I will scratch if it's scratching you want I will
red your neck in the loud night later I will
split your eyes you cage you mew you petted
name that lives in their mouths wet and easy
you cat

BENSON LAMENTS THE LOSS OF HEDGES

It was you that saw the glinting hooks, went *Yes*. Nothing new down here but that. The gold on me prickled.

You bit hooks like they were live meat, and let them drag you Up. You'd be dragged easily, quietly, like it was your last time and you were being dragged not by those bodies there above us, but just the Up's strong will itself. When they got you they'd hold you in those fronds of theirs, meaty and thick. And you quiet, still. I know that in you there was a squall of froth and churn and go back go back go back. Sitting perfectly still being cuddled, the Up nagging at your skin to get in. Always they'd slide you back in and in you'd glide, the bubbles behind you blank like nothing had happened, and you finding meat and swallowing it with your mouth mashed. I know you were hurting because I followed you, baby, we split that cool pain. Saw it three times with my mouth full of wormmeat before I came after you.

I followed the red line falling from your lip till you were there, moonsize and dragging me after you. Quietly we swallowed everything. The plants and the babyuns and the worms all the same. Your lip clotted then crabshelled, got as old as rocks are. Oh, you looked inedible. You flicked forwards gentle, and your body said *Be the biggest and the Up can't eat you. Come back from where nothing comes back from.*

We swelled and ate and my first hook was an accident. A raw singing suddenly in my lip and I thought, *Oh*. Fought it then thought of you. Rose unfightingly with grace. And then feeling the hot, calloused fronds from those big bodies that stick to the floor, sitting in the jaws of the Up, its dry breath on me and the slush of my insides gone mad, all my body hotting and begging me and the shadow of your body mute below me, the length of it spelling *Calm*. So I was, and lay frightened but not moving, the floorstickers touching the bigness of me, mooing in a way I now know means *Good, Lovely, Yes*. All of me fat and pretty with drips of the world flying off me. Your quiet shadow waiting. And then their fronds pushing me back down below and my old everything rushing to meet me, that good chill I'd been feeling all my life suddenly new, suddenly sweet. You came to me and off we glid, blood glinty in my mouth.

Baby, that's what our life tasted like. Red, frothy. Eating all of everything like we were twice the size of us. Swelling twice the size of us and swallowing more. You ramming into me when the sex took you. Us eating the eggs when I made em. Me following you, but you me sometimes. Nothing alive or shining we wouldn't take into our mouths. Our whiskers whipping all meat, the tinies, the flitters, the stickly babyun bugs, the floor's fronds green and dancing into our jaws. All of the floor for us and everything above it too. Hooks'd take you and I'd wait, thinking on you up there. Fierce and belly big over me, your mouth all coppery with pride.

Now I flick around, I float. I've laid so many eggs my insides roil with the hurt of it. Maybe I've had your babies, baby. Maybe I ate em. Can't know, not really. And still I bite a hook when I see it. The floorstickers different each time but still the same reverent moos, the same white slap back into the same world I left, the tedium of relief waiting to greet me. Oh baby I am so ashamed I want to live. Hard now to picture the patterns of you. Just your slow-moving shadow, long and cool, or sometimes your distant glint of gold. No way to know if you thought *Baby* too.

Sometimes death holds me so dry and tender it comes back like a rush of foam, what me and you was like. And then I'm flung back to the chill dark and I glide forward, mouth sore, open, my body huge and shining beautiful, and know that in all of the murk I am the only golden thing but there is nothing in it to see me.

WHO'S A GOOD BOY?

I am yes am good with a mouth full yes for you, the air's pee food body you you food body you and I am out and out and Oh that's the bad body in the air, you gimmeakick and ah, gotit –

used to be the black water spilled in me, I'd play till it drained, but you you've helped me not to, keep me cross and cold please yes please, and there he is, another you but bad, in my nose my ears in my soft parts he is loud, and I am loud in his for you, yes I am good I am loud I am cross I am yes I am yes I am yes

CAROLINE

There are countries where a romantic relationship with an animal is legal, such as Brazil, Mexico and Thailand, though it is difficult to move to these nations from the U.K. Becoming an ex-pat in one of the enlightened states of Nevada, New Hampshire, New Mexico, Texas, Vermont or Wyoming is perhaps even trickier – migration to the U.S. being nigh impossible without a tie to the States by marriage or blood.

At the time of writing the U.K. belongs to the E.U., and so it is for the moment simple for British citizens to relocate to Romania, Hungary, or Finland. However, finding English-language work in Human Resources there is challenging over the Inter-net.

Section 69, Subsection (2) of the 2003 Sexual Offences Act officially declares intentionally causing or allowing an animal to 'penetrate' you illegal. It is specified that the 'penetration' must be done with a penis, which excludes some other forms of romantic tenderness.

For an animal to board an aeroplane, vaccinations, microchipping, heartworm prevention and both flea and worming treatments are among the costs one incurs, alongside the additional payments individual airlines may arbitrarily add. Quotes vary, but favouring the highest estimates, this totals approximately £200 – a not insurmountable figure.

One caught in breach of Section 69, Subsection (2) of the 2003 Sexual Offences Act may face up to no more than 2 years of prison. It is noteworthy that among the available examples of such incarcerations, there is no noticeable difference in the sentencing of those who stated, under oath, that they were in love, and those who did not. Scandinavian studies state that in most cases, animals have suffered anxiety, fear, and physical trauma, often dying from their injuries, but they don't know what they're talking about.

WHITE TIGER FARM

Stripeless I'm the most loved   my brother orangestreaked he grew he went   I'm a new shape just for playing

the men with the buckets come and open my mouth for me   him straightbacked and hungry would have tore them   I am built too kind

hello the men shout a body through the door   not him marked and muscled and gonenow but another me   me I'm just for playing he's white not white as me though and with a bashedin face   brother would have gone to him skirling and flyblown not me   I'm lightbulbcoloured me I'm the loved one

thanks the men with the buckets thanks he comes to my spine singing   him that old wailing and blackbarred he'd have spoiled this   this new me climbs to play in the hollow my back's made for him hello

in the sore shadows we open our mouths ourselves and low   wherever my brother is I bet he is not even listening to this   slow white bothofme smacking while the men roar   at this shape that we have made   all of us   together

HOUNDS OF LOVE

Me Im th turbl crature
o th lake, llong drown now
n rot n et, rrr. I was dogsinbags
pitched in, a deep jostle
sinking arrowly, hullo. All come
in th lake come a part til all
slime tgethr. Bt jlust us singing,
hullo.

Skn n wrappngs gone awhilenow,
dowln here, but our blk tungsre
llivid, blk llips n rloofbones o
mlouths all tptptping
llow in th pooll thlat ylou llook at
rippleless wth th trees blk
n culuddling th edges.

Yes Im th stll brlown hart in th wds
lovng evrthng. Thlrobbing
thlrough th pines. Thumpn
twoofyou prlessn brlackn t yself
on my edges, dont be afraid.
Th hessian o me s waving,
round th mossy dogrib.
Beau t fl. Yes. Beau. Bu. B.

OUR CAT, CAT, ON HER LAST DAY

So many new places these days. He puts me in a box and lets me out in a new room. My empty insides moan.

A tall new body holds me, puts his fingers in my mouth. They are blue and smell of nothing. It hurts. Last night the little ones rubbed my back until I melted with calm.

I'm walked down a long corridor from mine. I look at mine. He looks at me.

New places these days. I'm sat down. Hands I hadn't noticed come from behind, hold me. My stomach roils. Too tired to fuss. There is a square of sunlight on the carpet, yellow and warm, and I decide *when I am let go, I will go to it.*

BAA

They're replacing all the animals with sheep. We can't have other animals anymore.

It starts with dogs. You had your chance with dogs. You're going to have a sheep waiting for you at home and a sheep to walk in the evenings and a sheep to pick up after with your hand in an inside-out plastic bag. Sheepdogs are just going to be sheep with ambition. Then the birds. Sheep reaching impotently for your birdbath, their pink mouths expectant. One crammed into your birdcage, squalling. And then rabbits and gibbons and all the rest of it.

Zoos are going to be underwhelming. Pits with sheep in. Cages with sheep in. Sheep quietly considering the tyre the elephants used to kick around. I don't know why we'll go. Aquariums will be worse. We will walk in the wobbly blue light of the tunnels, the huge tanks empty where the sharks used to play. Sheep floating silently above us like low clouds.

Finally they will replace the insects and we won't have room to move. The world white and coarse from the waist below, floor fading into obscurity. I will try and remember the tickle of grass on my back and fail. I will marvel at the memory of mud on your knees. You won't be able to hear me over the bleating. I will try to move to you and I will not be able to. Your fingers will slip from mine as I'm pulled away by the living riptide. I'm sorry. I love you. I will miss you so well.

Oh, sheep are better, that's why. Quiet and blank and their eyes are lightless. And when they do speak, they sound like they're grieving. That's important. The world will sing plaintively. Let's sleep outside tonight, touch our skin to the soil, print little silhouettes into the dirt. When they come for us, remember it, hard, and I'll remember it too, hard, in the few minutes before we're replaced by something perfect.

ACKNOWLEDGEMENTS

Versions of some of these poems were published in *The Morning Star, Poems in Which, Belleville Park Pages, DOGZPLOT*, Stirred Press and *Spork*. The poem 'In the Cat Café' owes much to David Hartley's excellent article on the subject, published in *The Skinny*.

Special thanks to noble land mammal Jasmine Chatfield, without whom this book would be very different, probably worse. Thanks also to Lenni Sanders, for her majestic and precise workshopping of early drafts, to Rachel Piercey and Emma Wright for helping this gross baby get born (the pamphlet, not me) and to Mark Andrew Webber for his killer-diller illustrations. I'm also very grateful to Anthony Trevelyan, Eoghan Walls and Emma Jane Unsworth, for kindly saying nice things about the poems for the blurb.

Finally, thanks to my Dad, for his help in rhyming 'bollocks' with 'scallops'.

ABOUT THE POET

Jack Nicholls comes from Cornwall. His fiction and poetry have been published in the *Chicago Quarterly Review, PANK, The Best New British and Irish Poets 2017* (Eyewear) and other places. He makes comedy with the sketch group Beach Hunks and runs the experimental live art event FLIM NITE in Manchester, where he's currently based.

ABOUT THE ILLUSTRATOR

Artist-printmaker Mark Andrew Webber specialises in painstakingly-researched typographic and geometric projects, including his 'Where in the World' series of enormous city maps and 'FORM', a six-part study of line and form. In 2007, Webber was awarded a Silver Cube award from the Art Directors Club of New York. His first solo exhibition, 'Wonderlust', was on display at the Londonewcastle Project Space in London in 2014. He collaborated with poet Jacqueline Saphra on her pamphlet *If I Lay on my Back I Saw Nothing but Naked Women* (Emma Press, 2014), illustrating her poems with linocuts inspired by his lifedrawing sketches. He is based in Reading.

The Emma Press

small press, big dreams

The Emma Press is an independent publisher dedicated to producing beautiful, thought-provoking books. It was founded in 2012 by Emma Wright in Winnersh, UK, and is now based in Birmingham. Having been shortlisted in both 2014 and 2015, the Emma Press won the Michael Marks Award for Poetry Pamphlet Publishers in 2016.

The Emma Press is passionate about making poetry welcoming and accessible. In 2015 they received a grant from Arts Council England to travel around the country with *Myths and Monsters*, a tour of poetry readings and workshops for children. They are often on the lookout for new writing and run regular calls for submissions to their poetry anthologies and pamphlet series.

Sign up to the Emma Press newsletter to hear about their upcoming events, publications and calls for submissions. Their books are available to buy from the online shop, as well as in bookshops.

https://theemmapress.com
http://emmavalleypress.blogspot.co.uk